Encouragement for a Man
Falling to His Death

Encouragement for a Man Falling to His Death

poems by
Christopher Kennedy

AMERICAN POETS CONTINUUM SERIES, No. 107

BOA Editions, Ltd ❧ Rochester, NY ❧ 2007

First Edition
07 08 09 10   7 6 5 4 3 2 1

Publications and programs by BOA Editions, Ltd.—a not-for-profit corporation under section 501 (c) (3) of the United States Internal Revenue Code—are made possible with the assistance of grants from the Literature Program of the New York State Council on the Arts; the Literature Program of the National Endowment for the Arts; the County of Monroe, NY; the Lannan Foundation for support of the Lannan Translations Selection Series; the Sonia Raiziss Giop Charitable Foundation; the Mary S. Mulligan Charitable Trust; the Rochester Area Community Foundation; the Arts & Cultural Council for Greater Rochester; the Steeple-Jack Fund; the Elizabeth F. Cheney Foundation; Eastman Kodak Company; the Chesonis Family Foundation; the Ames-Amzalak Memorial Trust in memory of Henry Ames, Semon Amzalak and Dan Amzalak; and contributions from many individuals nationwide.

See Colophon on page 72 for special individual acknowledgments.

Cover Design: Prime8Media
Cover Art: Peter Forbes
Interior Design and Composition: Richard Foerster
Manufacturing: Thomson-Shore
BOA Logo: Mirko

Library of Congress Cataloging-in-Publication Data

Kennedy, Christopher, 1955–
    Encouragement for a man falling to his death / by Christopher Kennedy. — 1st ed.
        p. cm. — (American poets continuum series ; no. 107)
    ISBN 978–1–929918–98–0 (pbk. : alk. paper) ISBN 978-1-934414-02-6 (alk. paper)
    I. Title.

PS3611.E557E53 2007
811'.6--dc22
                                    2007002630

BOA Editions, Ltd.
Nora A. Jones, Executive Director/Publisher
Thom Ward, Editor/Production
Peter Conners, Editor/Marketing
Glenn William, BOA Board Chair
A. Poulin, Jr., President & Founder (1938–1996)
250 North Goodman Street, Suite 306
Rochester, NY 14607
www.boaeditions.org

NATIONAL
ENDOWMENT
FOR THE ARTS

State of the Arts

NYSCA

This book is dedicated to the memory of my father,
James M. "Lefty" Kennedy

No death for you. You are involved.
—Weldon Kees

Table of Contents

I

II

III

I

The Alchemist's Lament

All I dream of is chemical changes, animals coaxed
into hybrid shapes, one shifting molecule
in a piece of metal. I squint to see the diamond glint
on a piece of unearthed coal. I long to invent
a framework for transcendence, the illusion
of flesh melted away, a man transformed
beyond the narcotic world. Yet I'm resigned
to failure, to the earth's inertia. I curse
the certainty of decay, the irrevocable loss of matter.
I open my eyes in the morning to find things in order,
the illusion of the bright earth exactly as it was
the day before. Still, I hold out hope for permutation,
like a man in his kitchen with the lights out,
opening the refrigerator door, about to enter a silver spaceship.

Speech Identification Procedure

The word *father* flew by like a wounded hawk, but I saw clearly the past, the present, and the future ploughed up: taste of a dying star.

A word can stand for an absence the way light stands for dead stars. A father can fly by like a bird and disappear in a copse of trees.

A person can stand still for a very long time while moving about in the world. My days are like this, a scarecrow in a field, trying to imagine *birds*.

The Criminal

Maybe it's the air being filled with itself, the train speaking a very different language, the cost of traveling too far a constant reminder in the back of your face that just sits there, the face a piece of flesh that would rather be something else, say, the front of a bank building or a map that everyone could read to find their way home, but your face is very much a face, very much a map that tells nothing to no one, that rides beside you in the window of the train all by itself, superimposed over the lifeless gray of Indiana and constantly turning as you turn, staring right at you like the criminal who boarded miles back, smiling at everyone from above his handcuffs, so that maybe he's making you feel this way, and he wants to trade faces with someone on this train and he's locked onto you, and everyone suspects you're not the person you were when you got on, and you can never hope to be the person who gets off, stops, and looks around like someone who is home, or very near to something like it.

                                                               ✍

Riddle of Self-Worth

By cannibal standards, I'm dinner for six.
My pet vulture has the disconcerting habit of staring
at the clock and then at me. In terms of sun,
I plan for a long Alaskan winter. Insurance salesmen
slink away from me at parties. A stiff breeze
blows away my weight in gold. In the world of before
and after, I remain steadfastly before. Last session,
my psychiatrist shook my hand and thanked me
for curing his insomnia. If I had a nickel for every time
my name was associated with greatness, I would owe
someone a quarter. My mother called recently and asked
for her umbilical cord. Yet I'm resilient, a human cockroach.
I'll be here for a while, blocking progress in a black leather jacket,
switchblade quick and ruthless as a jar of pennies.

∾

Death by Misadventure

The shards of last night's window remember
what it meant to be whole. A few stained-glass saints
lie disassembled in the grass. I hide behind a leafless tree,
camouflaged in my cat-hair suit, a pile of rocks
at my naked feet. The enemy waves each time they pass
the place where I pretend not to be. I lick the suit
where wounds occur. An officer of highest standing
orders his troops to open fire. I'm flattered for a moment
then overcome with the desire to surrender. The enemy
lowers their rifles. They look at me through bare branches
and smile. We wear the same uniform-that much is true-
though they see me as a different breed. It's only a matter
of time before I become an integral part of the conflict.
Meanwhile, the century turns, like a worm in an unmarked grave.

❧

Halfway Down the Wishing Well

A man has to see death several times
and like what he sees to pierce a hole
in his own heart. He has to be so afraid
that he has no fear. He has to stay up
all night, trying to stop the germ
of his loneliness from eating his insomnia.
The terrible idea of living has to wake him
from his lack of sleep, as he watches
the black clouds drift, like the hulls
of ghost ships, across his window's horizon.
He has to feel like a coin, tossed by a sweaty hand,
halfway down the wishing well.
He has to know love is a blood sport
and a godsend. He has to be sadder

than a river, winding its way toward an ocean
it can't see. He has to kneel down
at the river and sip from his own reflection.
He has to cross the river and spit in each
of Cerberus' six eyes. He has to spook
the moon with the howling of his brain.
He has to love his own ghost. He has to be
a man of conviction in an era of who gives
a fuck. He has to bleed, like a rabbit
in his den of dreams. There can be nothing left
for him to do except curse the devil and spurn
any notion of chicken-shit heaven. And pull
the cold sheet over himself, like a blanket
of snow over the graves of the violent dead.

⨎

Edward Hopper's Dream

I found myself asleep in a white hotel,
sunlight bullying me awake. Sunlight pressing against
my back, shoving me out of bed. A nude woman
lumbered ghostly from wall to wall, her head bowed
chin to chest. Outside, a green window box with red geraniums.
Another nude woman was there, pumping gas.
A small brushfire in the distance. Jackson Pollock drove by,
his car in flames. I felt ashamed of America
but also in love with it. My head turned to sand and began
to sift through my fingers. Yes, I forgot. I stood there
with my head in my hands, weary as a priest.
In the next moment I was awake again, riding in an automobile.
A green cast to the car. Heading somewhere along the Cape.
Though the towns we passed all looked like Nyack.

Aria

No sunrise but the orange on the table;
pleasure in the form of a black dog. The spider's
red insistence collaborates with a yellow sponge
to form the morning's art. A fly crawls
toward the light fixture, an opaque white etched with gold
and blue seraphim. I set the roses on fire in the sink;
I watch the flames and smell the scent of burning petals.
I hear the cat cries of murder and sense the mole's reality.
What I think is not relevant; invisible as a concept,
blind as paper. The ether-shine evokes a day of penitence,
an unremembered memory of scent, the balsam hour
of sex. I understand the need for fresh air
and open the window to breathe, just in time
to hear the singing of small children I can't see.

Loveliest of Zombies

I have plans, archetypes, blueprints,
trapezoidal structures, dug from the ruins
of my last love affair. Or rather, the last time
I touched flesh it withered, rotted, turned
sundry shades of yellow and blue.
There's something beautifully unnatural about you,
too, a corpse-like pall that suggests *indoor fluorescence*,
a "B" Movie sheen that screams out to me
from the red gash of your lips. You're stitched tight,
an assemblage of Old World parts that evokes
an ominous castle in a storm. Given all this,
can I expect a quick reply? Is it mutual like rain
agreeing to be rain? I hope not. I'm dressed
too old for the weather. I love you as if you were dead.

Blue Collar Drive

My father steered me past the steel mill where he worked. Drove through a mountain of fog. When we emerged: pedestrian traffic; sheenless buildings. A mountain of stones for boys to throw as punishment, until the mountain exists on the other side of the street.

Rain dripped up the car window; white smoke from the refinery ribboned its way toward a vacant heaven. The light turned green as predicted. The used car took its magic turn.

❦

My Father's Work Clothes

Reduced to memory, a torn blue work shirt and pants worn through at the knees. At night, I'm secretly trying to mend them, my seven-year-old fingers fumbling with the needle, but I have no thread, and my hands keep folding, mysteriously, into prayer.

On Earth, As It Is in Heaven

Pale clouds conceal
the night's black appetite.
Ensconced in moonlight,
the apparition of the trees.

The bare patch
in the northeast corridor:
an eye socket
in the century's skull.

Tomorrow hides
in a little satchel,
its hopes not unlike
our own: to arrive.

I wake up early
in a new paradigm of fear:
the stars glint like the tips
of a thousand knives.

Plato's Bar and Grill

Clock of fake ivory, radio music, mostly static
and bass, the clink of glass on glass. Here
all arguments speak of Archimedes, and I wonder
about a body's weight imbued with fluids, if it displaces
more of the air around it or if it sinks deeper into itself.
I look out toward the tables' flat horizons, wanting to know
if the world ends there, while patrons sit and wait
for night to extinguish, their heads canted slightly down,
like a chorus of true and melancholy Greeks.
One by one each raises a finger toward a harried waitress,
who nods a quick acknowledgment. I leave them
where they sit, hopeful the next round brings clarity,
and turn my attention to the flicker of beer lights from behind
the bar, as on the wall drunken silhouettes begin to dance.

The Porous Umbrella

When it rains, I grab my porous umbrella and stand outside on the street. I stroll along with all the others, our umbrellas raised over our heads until the street becomes a garden of damp black flowers. I love the feel of water as it filters through the tiny holes and lands on my shoulders. And I know how to project the appearance of a man who knows exactly what to do when the sky opens up above his head and the heavens send a replenishing downpour.

I highly recommend you buy your own. Unless you're the reckless type with no regard for how you're perceived. Then I suggest you stand in the rain and be thought a fool or follow the herd with their intact parasols, while I create the illusion that I'm dry. But I say join me in my surreptitious drench, and I'll teach you the secret of my holey shoes.

Sunflowers

I drove along the highway and saw a field of sunflowers. Above them hovered all of television's fine-featured angels, beatific, hair of spun gold. Then the fallen angels appeared, straight from the bowels of hell, wings of black leather, angry, bat-like faces, and they began to devour the delicate angels, and the field became a killing field, the sunflowers' orange blossoms seeped red with angel blood. And from the blood grew a new kind of flower, its bloom a giant thorn, hooked like a claw. It rose higher than the sunflowers, almost piercing a low cloud. And Allah spoke to Buddha, and Buddha spoke to Yahweh, and Yahweh spoke to Christ, and Christ spoke to Vishnu, and a nervous whispering occurred in all the different heavens that penetrated each fragile human ear.

❧

Vesper

After the funeral, I heard the faint ringing of a small-mouthed bell in the tower of a white church. A sinner, I was called to the evening prayer, dumbstruck and almost deaf. That I could hear at all was a miracle or a testament to the bell's simple clarity and the clear summer air.

I decided to follow, like a pilgrim, the slow path toward righteousness. I donned my sackcloth and flagellated myself until my back began to burn and ache. Before I knew it, two sharp bones cut through my shoulder blades and sprouting wings unfurled.

That's as close as I got to flight. I bound the wings behind me, because I knew the myth, the father's good intentions and the son, spiraling downward into the sea.

⇌

Work Ethic

With maps torn and outdated,
I arrive where X marks the spot.
Falling to my knees, I dig
with bare hands for buried treasure.
Unprepared, the boyhood motto
of the working class, stitched
on my lapel. For years, I displace
the various strata, a mound of clay
and rock above the hole where I stay
bent to task. Just as I'm ready
to give up, out of jokes that refer to China,
my fingertips scrape against a solid object.
I'm in before I recognize it:
a cedar box, surface bucked with roses.

❧

Dead Horse

It had been dead for years. The others beat it as if it would jump to its feet and ride off. I saddled it sideways and slid on. There was nowhere to go, and I had the perfect means. The others kept pounding their fists against the rotten hide, expecting an unlikely response. They managed the illusion of a galloping hoof, but only for a moment. They looked at me as if I could tell them what to do next. I set my gaze on the horizon and rode hard in ways too difficult to explain.

II

To the Man Who Played the Violin and Fell from a Plank into a Vat of Molten Steel

They buried an ingot instead of a man,
a cry encased in steel to replace a soul,
the faux soul trapped and singing of liquid fire.
There are buildings built with him
inside their beams. His story: A man fell
into a molten sea and the sea returned a city.
Here's another story: The man played
the violin; he gave his friend who played the fiddle
a grapevine that grew behind the friend's house,
and every summer day the friend's son
looked out his window at the vine that grew
untrellised and watched the wild birds eat
the grapes that dried in the afternoon sun.

The son would try to imagine what
the man's last thought might have been,
and he could never find the words to make
a thought that would capture
whatever a man would think at the moment
the unthinkable was happening.
And the story of the man stayed with the son,
who asked his mother to tell it to him
whenever the son missed his father,
who died when the boy was young.
And every time the mother would say,
Your father worked with a man from Portugal
who played the violin, and one day at work,
he fell from a plank into a vat of molten steel.

Duration of the Spider

Though spider is my nature,
I aim toward human urges and shape
my face to suit the mood around me.
I stick to corners and wait,
my web strewn with stunned buzz.
Silent, I hope for redemption,
but I know damnation lurks at the end
of a lizard's blue tongue
or a frightened child's hand. A simple flick
from nowhere, and I cease to be.
At night, I wait for a finger
to switch the harsh light into existence
and pray, when judgment comes, to ransom
my weight with the currency of dead flies.

Encouragement for a Man Falling to His Death

I'm sorry your parachute is made of cream cheese, but think of the spectators and their stories, and the asphalt's loneliness until you arrive, abruptly and without pretense. You've heard of Jesus; now you get to be just like Him. Every eye that holds your image belongs to a person who will know, once and for all time, what it means to be alive. Those who loved you most will place a wreath at the exact spot where you became an exact spot. Footage of your fall will serve as effective warning to all who believe cream cheese to be a healthy substitute for silk. I hope this isn't too much for you to learn on your return to our distant planet, where all is well as well as all is not so well, depending on where you're headed, the east and west of which you probably never stop to consider, obsessed as you are with the physics of north and south.

❧

King Cobra Does the Mambo

Mad provocateurs, your monocles are bull's eyes
in prosthetic heaven. The sky reeks of neutrinos
and crows. Days are serpentine. Gold is priceless;
the moon a worthless stone. Manufacturers
suggest the luminous coloratura of ad agencies
as crippled blood coagulates in shrines, the Lourdes
of which is unknown. Mastodons of long extinction
rise from the tar pits to say, *I love you,*
but you never phone. For this, our species waited centuries.
That's as far as I go today; the chores of destiny
can wait. Maybe it's me. Maybe the tongues
of my shoes have taken over. When I walk,
people listen. When I dream, I intuit the laughter
of trees. That, or a runaway train headed your way.

❧

Exits

Another night spent burning the empty calories of love. The solicitude of hands brings comfort for a while. My tongue swells on your skin's smooth arena. Tiny rivers of sweat form on our brows, and I think of the sea and Carthage in ruins, the salt-smell of whatever passes between us. The gods smile, and it's hard to tell whose side they've chosen. Or if they bother to choose. The future endures, for a moment, without us. The chill starts in me and ends in you: death. For a moment, everything. Then, nothing. I could listen to your heart all night, knowing it will stop. This is love. This is how it ends, praying, in darkened rooms, it never ends.

Life Cycle

How many centuries flew by like startled birds,
I'll never know, but the earth teemed
with modern cities by the time I was awake.
This wasn't a dream. It was a life
in which a dream is a small part and means
almost nothing. Now I was the earth's shadow,
a penumbra, still, in the swirling dust
of the exploded universe, waiting to be reborn.
It seems I had a choice, the kind no one
tells you about until you're a tree,
rooted in the soil, trying to scream your roots
and branches free. That's the wind at night
when you're a child, wide awake in bed,
counting the strange thoughts you thought were stars.

Myth

I asked for a fact instead of a resurrection. I was given a slap and an ink stain to clean that grows bigger every day. Each morning I find a white towel and scrub, but the spot spreads larger. I never think to ask for help. I still don't know if that's a sign of strength or weakness. I can't even tell if I'm alive or dead and waiting to return. At night, when the stain covers the blue sky, you'll know my failure. Stars glint where I poke through. That should give you hope. A full moon means I've worked hard. Don't let the sun fool you. I'm busy on the other side of the world.

Poor Excuse

My head began to fill with a mixture of concrete and helium. I drifted heavily above the earth. It was as it always is. I was far above and feeling unsure. My ego stuck in a small air pocket where helium displaced concrete.

I saw my mother, pinning my father's ghost on a gray rope between two silver poles.

It's hard to impart the fear of mooring inappropriately on someone's clothesline, another faded unmentionable.

Then I thought to anchor myself with the help of a Good Samaritan. I called out to every passerby to grab my ankles. Only children responded. All of them too short, following along below me.

They were thought to be frivolous by those who watched from their windows. I was considered a poor excuse for a parade.

⤳

The Man in the Kangaroo

I was born a plastic doll with fluttering eyelids, my door totally off its hinges, under the affluent rays of the moon. At first, I felt uneasy, like a man who sleeps ten minutes from a tornado, dreaming of trains.

When my father drove a borrowed car to heaven, I waited at the rain-streaked window for a lifetime. To adapt to my situation, I transmogrified my synthetic innards to a replica of a human soul.

My mother taught me that trick on her knee, while she played a skeleton tuned to sound like a banjo. Daily, I scurried for her pouch, but she was strict and splayed me under the brilliant sun.

I'm adjusted now, less easily spooked, and almost always entertained. Rain, however, seems more mysterious than ever.

There is no story here to tell. I'm a type of fog, the pre-thought trance of a cold baby left to die on a mountainside in Thebes.

᷑

Political Poem

I spoke to an audience comprised entirely of gerbils about issues surrounding sunflower seeds and their distribution, and they were rapt, running as they were on their pointless wheels. I mentioned the wood chip shortage, and they stopped, and I could sense the tide turning against me. When I finished, I took the lack of applause as a cultural difference and left the dais to the chirping of a new constituency of crickets.

&

San Francisco: 1978

The mayor rested in a pool of martyr blood,
but a thinner corpse stole the spotlight.
Street gangs straddled their motor-machines,
each face lit up with candle-flame.
The folk singer told us to go home; our grief
was not her kind of grief. That was my own
personal gunshot wound: *Slump.* The governor's reprieve
arrived an hour too late. I was streaked
with afterthoughts, the cold press of the rain.
A newsboy shouted *Earthquake in Mexico City!*
I felt a tremor beneath me and walked to the nearest sanctuary.
I leaned in to sip when an entire herd of impatient waitresses
approached the watering hole. *I was born pink*, I said,
as if I could stem the inevitable tide.

Serial Killer Blue

The sky makes good use of space. Its blue void teaches the lesson of the day. Birds use it as a backdrop when they're feeling dramatic. It is their sea, also. There's no reason why a person can't look up and say *The gulls are swimming east today.* Unless, of course, they're headed west.

Age of Transcendence

A nervous, mildewed child, I was less afraid of ghosts
before my father became one. I ate what I was fed
and lay all night in the hooded dark, listening to the house breathe.
I was never healed by the sound of wind through trees,
the row of poplars, swaying at the end of the field,
and I listened hard for the rush of traffic in the distance headed away.
When I grew older, I purchased handfuls of extraction dust,
determined to push my soul past the limits of my skin.
Bone-sculpture, skinnier than wire, I loved my murderers.
I loved my murderers, my friends, who loved me, too,
all of us seduced by the same impossible desire to leave
our bodies. I was afraid of ghosts, but I loved the end
of the world, the idea of sitting on a hill, watching the cloud
in the distance, one small step from the moon.

❧

The Mother I Never Had

The exaggerated strain of my conscience calls to me in the morning when I venture to the floor, feet first to shower. The wavering patterns of the wood grain resemble foreign shores.

The tourist in me goes crazy, if only for a moment. Then the cold of winter reminds me where I really am.

I raise one hand to shade my eyes and look out the window at the sun: a yellow plate on a blue tablecloth.

Smoke rises from a chimney and hangs in the nearly frozen air. I see the gentle face of the mother I never had, smiling through a Valium haze. I could stand here, motionless, posed for eternity.

This is how statues are made.

III

My Father in the Fifth Dimension

Once I attended the burning of a house.
Late October, and each flame-tipped leaf
that flew past threatened to set me on fire.
A crowd gathered, and I watched as a secret
tried to burn its way out of everyone's flame-stunned faces.
I wouldn't learn what it was until much later.
The house was too young to die. It was my father,
the secret, only I didn't know it then.
He was the house, too. But since I thought
it was only a house, I watched it burn.
It didn't become my father until years later
when every presence became his absence:
the moon in its phases, the tireless leaves
dropping to the ground, the russet-colored horse
that keeps its head down in a photo from another century—
my father, also. He is timeless, traveling
in the tightest imaginable circle on a curve
located on a cylinder beneath an invisible plane.
I visit there in dreams. One time, during a long visit,
my spine slithered out of a slit at the base
of my neck. Like a skinned-snake, it wriggled away
until I picked it up. Then it turned into a guitar,
and with it I struck the chord of dissonance
and woke up to the sound of distant thunder.
I was the train in Magritte's *Time Transfixed*,
floating out of the fireplace, without tracks
or destination. It was at this moment the infinite
seemed possible. I closed my eyes. I heard a voice
as near and remote as childhood, saying *You live
in a country where no one speaks the language.
Rely on the body.* It was then I became the father
of a great desire. I wanted to put my head

on my mother's pillow, to feel the smooth,
curved beads of her rosary, strung in decades
on a silver chain. But sleep is no substitute
for death, or rather the life after death,
so I woke up from the dream within the dream
and set out to find a burning house, the moon,
some fallen leaves, a horse from another century.

☙

Blind Man's Photographs

What is the night, except an excuse not to see? The dim lamps of memory are no use; even the stars can't light up an entire sky. My life, like a blind man's photographs strewn carelessly around his room; figures blurred, streaks of light and shade, composition left to chance. A picture for each day. The day you leave: unusual shadows on the ground; a flock of giant scissors overhead.

Dusk

Leaves fall like red ash from a burning building, and the wind whisks them away. A rabid dog runs the ditch with the rest of the pack. I watch the twin girls across the street hurl their bodies like stones against the mirror of each other's face. A red car, painted with an Aztec bird, screams by beyond the speed limit. The air smells of smoke and rain. The earth seems to tremble with rage. History polishes its boots. A jumbled newspaper blows across my lawn like a wanted poster in a Western film, and the night comes down, final and certain, shiny black.

Moon, Father

Blue ash falls from your lips and a small cloud
settles in a tree. It's almost forever, and you still
haven't seen me. Though life beneath your fullness
bears little resemblance to death, the calcifying leaves
shuffling in the nearly calm moment this night delivers
might make me think of dying, but seeing you, I'm sure
that like the leaves you are never really gone, that you come
and go in phases. Still, the poplars sway and enter your stillness,
and I am frightened because there is a way you move
when I take off my glasses that leaves me believing
you never moved, since when you do, it's slow, like a child's life
to other children, and I press the meaning of death
upon you, not by logic, but by grief, and give you a name
that means *to fade*. Yours is the name that means to fade.

Herald

I yelled to them to stop humbling, but the police
recorded it as a threat. I am always only the sum
of my parts, the sliding scale of indifference.
I would, if time permitted, borrow your moth-wings
and fly straight toward the flame, but that's impractical,
like a steel window or a glass automobile,
and it's not just sardonic ambulances and ecstatic laundry,
I loved you as much if not more than any bicycle.

Perhaps you've mistaken me for your shoes again.
I'm not obsequious, just starving for reptiles,
but you wouldn't understand that craving.
Damn your categories! I'm only blooming flowers
of dark persuasion, a one-of-a-kind breed,
a thorny petal, the mold inside those shoes.

Ego Fugue

The green fly declared itself against the yellow curtain, rubbing its wicked, spindly legs. I was captured in the prisms of its segmented eyes. Reflected there, the various selves of my being separated like colors in a spectrograph. Each self a part of the greater self, a lurid, un-evolved aspect of what I aspire to be. I wondered out loud if this is what God had in mind when he created the universe. The fly accused me of blasphemy and buzzed off toward the ceiling, where I knew a spider lurked with hungry mouths to feed.

Dressed for Church

When you get far enough away to see where you've been, it's always smaller, your father is there, swimming in a small pond, like a sunfish you caught in the St. Lawrence Seaway when you were six. And it's not as if you can circle around and come up on it from the back, see it again, large as life. It recedes as you walk, compressing into a pinprick of light. And then your mother stands next to the clothesline with the wicker laundry basket in her hands, all your father's white shirts, hanging like ghosts from the lines. And then she's gone. The shirts flap in the wind a little, and you think of wounded soldiers begging mercy in the snow and turn and walk a bit farther, fascinated by the unlikely sheen of your new shoes.

❧

Progress

I'm learning to tell time by the shadow
on the blank wall where the broken clock used to be.
It was easier when it was always 7:20,
but I'm all for progress. It's harder at night,
of course, when the absence of shadow
forces me to guess. Given my flair for the dramatic,
I spend a lot of time warning my wife.
It's almost midnight! I say with a sense of urgency
usually reserved for undertakers or accountants.
And she ignores me, because it's never that late,
and even if it were, she can't understand
what there is to fear. *Fear itself,* I quote to her,
and she smiles the way one smiles at a child
who has lost its way and doesn't know it.

Broadway Lament

A dance of walls agitates the meadows
and America drowns itself in machines and lament.
—Federico García Lorca

This town has its share
of addictions, so if the rain
smells a little like whiskey,
I'm not imagining things.

On the fractured sidewalk
newspapers, billowy and disheveled,
sail by, and a few half-smoked cigarettes
ride the crest of a wave, stirred
by a street cleaner's broom—
the spume and tide of dereliction.

It's hard to believe I could be
considered the strange one here
among the pornographic faces
etched out of something less
than human kindness.

Jesus walked like this among
the whores and murderers,
trying to save their souls.

I'm here because fear is the only thing
I still respect that still respects me.

This is what people mean
when they say they're lonely.

Where I am the orangey,
high-gloss covers of dirty magazines
get their sheen, and invisible machines
drown me in their solicitude.

When a phone rings, I answer it,
even if I know it's not for me,
because the etiquette for these hours
has never been written in a book,
and if there's a voice out there
beyond the endless staff of quarter notes,
the streetlights that go on and off
like music, I'd like to hear it sing
a lament made popular in other corners
of the universe, a peripatetic blues
that wails through the radio waves
to secret government agencies
and begins: Curse on the moon,
the footsteps of man.

But there is little chance this song
will be sung, that a sound will emerge
from within the steady, familiar hum
of the machines, or if it does, that anyone
will hear it. Little chance that an out-
of-this-world strain of pure blues
could hit the right notes at this hour,
in this place, where all the stores are closed,
the ancient rhythm of my feet
the only music that carries me.

Reckless Journey

There's no real direction, and the road signs
are vague. There's a vast horizon and a sunset
bleeding red. The rest is a superfluous truck stop
of dubious origin. A couple of rig jockeys
straight out of central casting, sipping java in a booth.
Each soul that passes sings a song of country blues.
There's a smile on everyone's face, but no one seems happy.
Every dog barks as if it knows it has no bite.
It's strange to be a stranger in this strange land,
a peripatetic soul in the world of the living dead.
No choice now but to face it head on. My right thumb's
all I've got. I'm all highway and no town. It's raining,
and the roads are slick, there's a semi bearing down,
its twin beams of heaven the light at the end of my tunnel.

Broken Saints

The morning of my father's funeral, I stayed home and bit the heads off plastic statues, one after another until there was a pile of heads on one side of the room and a stack of headless bodies on the other. I quit at ten severed heads. I was very young, and I had given up hope that the babysitter would ever arrive.

Then I arranged the headless bodies like bowling pins and rolled the heads at them until all the bodies fell down. I did this through the morning, while the rest of the family attended the funeral. Then the babysitter arrived. I had been wrong to give up hope. She took me by the hand and asked me what game I was playing. When she saw the statues she shook her head.

She sat me down on the floor, and we began matching heads to bodies, gluing them together. The key, I learned, was eyeing the uneven necklines to see where the curves would mesh. They were never exact; the heads bowed slightly at times as if in prayer. And no matter how many times I tried, I couldn't hide their shame.

⇌

Better, Thanks

It was always hard for them to tell
which was foreign and which was domestic.
Also, who should wash the dancers,
who should interrogate the chicken.

Then there was the issue of who should steer
the weasel. He kept giving her directions
to the swimming pool. She argued the size
of his snowshoes. Once they arrived

wherever it was they were going, he would ratchet
the moon from the sky and offer it to her;
she would repair the shriveling skyscape.
They were so much in love with tomorrow, it never came.

And who can endure the litany of now? Return
the moon to its rightful owners. That's all I'm saying.

❧

Fire in the Match Factory

A careless security guard flicks a cigarette on the floor. Sparks catch the neat stacks of boxes, their familiar red, white, and blue: fire, cloud, sky. A million small particulars ignite, blazing as one great conflagration, a five-alarm inferno. I stand mute, a casual observer, unable to speak my own language. In the distance, the fire brigade queues with buckets of holy water in a futile attempt to douse the flames. Someone shouts, *Fight fire with fire*, and soon there's flames surrounding flames. All I can do is watch it burn. I hear the chief say, *It's a shame, but it was only a matter of time*. A man of the cloth replies, *That's heresy*. I repent, torn between two extremes, and turn my flame-shadowed face away.

Sense

Waiter, where is the fly I ordered
for my soup? Oh, snug
at the bottom of the bowl,
his bloated body eschewing wings.

I see. There's a sense to that
I understand, a fatal dissonance
that I admire. His choice conveys
a certain dignity, a way of seeing

beyond the world of flesh
that I can't help but envy.
When you spoon his Buddha-body out,
lifeless but serene, tell him

I salute his difficult decision to drown,
despite my own desire to swim.

The Afterlife

My wife's face is the color
of a moth. Soon, she will be sitting
in the next room with a stranger
who will hypnotize her. Her dreams
will pour forth like scarves in a stiff breeze
and gather into a seamless garment,
one the doctor wears, one that says you're cured,
you can go home now, lead a normal life.

When we leave, it is cold. The air
is indistinguishable from the invisible sunlight.
We are naked. We have grown wings.
The past is far away. From a distance,
it seems peaceful here. We begin to fly.
Nothing can stop what happens next.

Yes and No as Usual

In memory: M. H.

In the morning, I have the embarrassing habit
of embracing the air as if it were a long-lost father.
My favorite antelopes pull my chariot
of bones, my grip held tight on reigns
of mint-flavored floss. All before me
frozen tundra and refrigerator salesmen.
I survey the ruins of future civilizations,
like a prophet whose time has come and gone.
I resist the urge to say I told you so,
but only because I'm completely alone.
Alas, the flat world calls me to its sunset edge,
a blend of unearthly pink and orange.
I'm lured toward its predictable beauty.
Are we there yet? you might ask.

Acknowledgments

Grateful acknowledgment is made to the editors of the following print and online journals in which these poems first appeared, some in different versions:

Alphabet Faucet: "Blue Collar Drive";
America: "My Father's Work Clothes";
Corresponding Voices: "Loveliest of Zombies," "Sense," "Dressed for Church," "Dead Horse," "Plato's Bar and Grill";
Cream City Review: "Broadway Lament";
Fourteen Hills: "Encouragement for a Man Falling to His Death";
Grand Street: "On Earth, As It Is in Heaven";
Luna: "Blind Man's Photographs," "Moon, Father";
The Nebraska Review: "Exits";
The Quarterly: "The Afterlife";
PP/FF: An Anthology: "The Porous Umbrella";
Slope: "Poor Excuse," "The Alchemist's Lament," "Riddle of Self Worth";
Stone Canoe: "King Cobra Does the Mambo," "Life Cycle," "Speech Identification Procedure";
The Threepenny Review: "The Criminal";
THRIFT Poetry Journal: "Death by Misadventure."

Some of these poems appear in the chapbooks, *King Cobra Does the Mambo* and *"B" Sides*, from M2 Press.

Love and thanks to my wife, Mi, for reading draft after draft of the poems in this book and for caring about what I do.

Thanks to Peter Conners, Thom Ward, and all the folks at BOA for giving me the opportunity to publish this book, and special thanks to Peter for his editorial insights and suggestions.

Thanks to Brad Armstrong, Kevin Keck, Tobin O'Donnell, and Jeff Parker for their help along the way.

Thanks to my friends and colleagues at Syracuse—Michael Burkard, Arthur Flowers, Mary Gaitskill, Gerry Greenberg, Brooks Haxton, Mary Karr, Gregg Lambert, George Saunders, and Bruce Smith—for their support over the years.

Love and thanks to Sarah Harwell for being such a good reader and friend.

Love and thanks to Steph Scheirer for her friendship all these long years.

And love to my daughters, Tessa and Margeaux.

The Weldon Kees epigraph is from "The Smiles of the Bathers," from *The Collected Poems of Weldon Kees*, Donald Justice, Editor, University of Nebraska Press (1975): 44.

The epigraph for "Broadway Lament" is from Federico García Lorca's poem, "Ode to Walt Whitman," from *The Selected Poems of Federico García Lorca*, Francisco García Lorca and Donald M. Allen, Editors, New Directions (1955): 135.

❧

About the Author

Christopher Kennedy is the author of two previous full-length collections of poetry, *Trouble with the Machine* (Low Fidelity Press) and *Nietzsche's Horse* (Mitki/Mitki Press), and three chapbooks, *King Cobra Does the Mambo* (M2 Press), *"B" Sides* (M2 Press), and *Greatest Hits* (Pudding House).

A founding editor of the literary journal *3rd Bed*, he was born and raised in Syracuse, New York. He has worked as a janitor, a journalist, a stock boy, a salesman, a youth center director, a garbage man, a glass-cutter, a juvenile detention center counselor, a record store clerk, and an audiovisual aide. He is an associate professor at Syracuse University where he directs the MFA Program in Creative Writing.

BOA Editions, Ltd.
American Poets Continuum Series

Colophon

The Isabella Gardner Poetry Award is given biennially to a poet in mid-career with a new book of exceptional merit. Poet, actress, and associate editor of *Poetry* magazine, Isabella Gardner (1915–1981) published five celebrated collections of poetry, was three times nominated for the National Book Award, and was the first recipient of the New York State Walt Whitman Citation of Merit for Poetry. She championed the work of young and gifted poets, helping many of them to find publication.

The publication of this book is made possible, in part,
by the special support of the following individuals:

Anonymous (6)
Nancy & Alan Cameros
Gwen & Gary Conners
Susan DeWitt Davie
Peter & Sue Durant
Pete & Bev French
Dane & Judy Gordon
Kip & Deb Hale
Robin & Peter Hursh
Rosemary & Lew Lloyd
Stanley D. McKenzie
Boo Poulin
Deborah Ronnen
Mike & Pat Wilder
Glenn & Helen William